colleges and universities. The College Board has commissioned one of the nation's leading experts on financing higher education to assist the education community with gaining a better understanding of the challenges we now face. Jim is Vice President for Enrollments, Placement, and Alumni Affairs at the University of Rochester and is widely respected for his contributions on the subject.

I hope you find this monograph helpful as we look forward together to another challenging, yet successful, academic year. Best wishes.

Sincerely,

Wayne A. Locust
Director of Admissions

WAL:jms

University of Rochester
Rochester, New York 14627
(716) 275-3221
Fax: (716) 461-4595

UNIVERSITY OF
ROCHESTER

December 14, 1992

Ms. Laura Clark
Director of College Guidance
Riverdale Country Day School
5250 Fieldston Road
Bronx NY 10471

Dear Ms. Clark:

As you well know, it is our practice at the University of Rochester to keep you informed of noteworthy events, new program and academic offerings, and the activities of distinguished members of the Rochester family. In keeping with this tradition, I am pleased to present to you a signed copy of **The Effect of Financial Aid on Admissions and Enrollment** by Jim Scannell.

The cost of higher education has become a most difficult issue for families as well as

The Effect of Financial Aid Policies on Admission and Enrollment

Happy Reading

The Effect of Financial Aid Policies on Admission and Enrollment

James J. Scannell

Vice President for Enrollments, Placement and Alumni Affairs, University of Rochester

College Entrance Examination Board, New York

The College Board is a nonprofit membership organization committed to maintaining academic standards and broadening access to higher education. Its more than 2,700 members include colleges and universities, secondary schools, university and school systems, and education associations and agencies. Representatives of the members elect the Board of Trustees and serve on committees and councils that advise the College Board on the guidance and placement, testing and assessment, and financial aid services it provides to students and educational institutions.

In all of its book publishing activities the College Board endeavors to present the works of authors who are well qualified to write with authority on the subject at hand and to present accurate and timely information. However, the opinions, interpretations, and conclusions of the authors are their own and do not necessarily represent those of the College Board; nothing contained herein should be assumed to represent an official position of the College Board or any of its members.

Copies of this book are available from your local bookseller or may be ordered from College Board Publications, Box 886, New York, New York 10101-0886 at $10.95.

Editorial inquiries concerning this book should be directed to Editorial Office, the College Board, 45 Columbus Avenue, New York, New York 10023-6992.

Copyright © 1992 by College Entrance Examination Board. All rights reserved. The College Board, SAT, and acorn logo are registered trademarks of the College Entrance Examination Board.

Library of Congress Catalog Number: 92-081299

ISBN: 0-87447-451-5

Printed in the United States of America

Contents

Foreword ix
Introduction 1

1. The Emergence of Financial Aid in U.S. Higher
Education 3

The History of Financial Aid 3
Federal Involvement 4
The History of Need Analysis 9
A Standardized Procedure 10
A Question of Judgment 11
Access and Choice 12
Choice 13

2. The Evolution of Financial Aid Policies and
Practices 15

Conclusion 20

3. Institutional Need for Financial Aid 23

Higher Education, The American Dream 23
  Relationship of Aid and Costs 24
  Effect on Students 28
  The "Needy" Middle Class 29
Recruitment and Financial Aid 31
  Enrollment Management 31
  Effect on Financial Aid 32

4. Our Dual System of Higher Education: Sector Differences and Sector Similarities 35

  Competition? 38

5. Financial Aid: How Much Is Too Much? How Little Is Too Little? 39

Packaging 39
  Uniform Self-Help 40
  Self-Help Varied by Ability to Borrow 41
  Self-Help Varied by Desirability 42
  Self-Help Varied by Ability to Borrow and Desirability. . . . 42
  Admit/Deny 43
  Aid-Conscious Admission 44
  Merit Awards 44
  Renewals 45
  Other Approaches 45
Creative Management of Institutional Aid Budgets 47
  Scenario One 48
  Scenario Two 48
Programs that Work in Reverse 49
Strategy Summary 51

Contents

6. Targeting Financial Aid to Enrollment Goals 53

Calculating Enrollment Yields 54

More Empirical Research 57

7. Conclusions and Recommendations 67

References 69

Foreword

Each year, nearly one and a half million students across the country move directly from secondary school to the more than 3,000 colleges and universities in the nation. In addition, thousands of students enter higher education following a period of work or military service. This process whereby millions of young men and women annually choose, or are chosen by, colleges has been aptly described as "the great sorting."

In 1988, the College Board set out to conduct a comprehensive review of this great sorting—how students are distributed and distribute themselves across the variety of institutions of higher education in the United States—in an effort both to determine the extent to which the process serves the interests of students and institutions and, indeed, of the nation, and to demystify for parents and students the often-bewildering set of admission practices and procedures that mark the transition to college.

With the advice of professionals and experts in counseling, admission, financial aid, curriculum articulation, public policy, and professional associations, the *College Board Study of Admission to American Colleges and Universities in the 1990s* encompasses two series of monographs. The "Selective Admission Series," conceived by our colleague Fred A. Hargadon, Dean of Admission at Princeton University, and conducted under his leadership, addresses issues with particular implications for the more selective institutions (or, as Dean Hargadon has suggested, "institutions that engage in the process of selecting a class") and for the students who attend them. Recognizing that the majority of college-bound students attend a greater variety of institutions of higher education than those represented in the first group, the "Admission Practices Series" addresses additional issues of importance and concern to the educational community as a whole and the public at large. The two series are closely related and integral to the study.

During its history, the College Board has played an instrumental role in promoting consensus on ways to improve the efficiency, effectiveness, and fairness of the system of admission to college and the processes that surround that system. At a time when the means by which students find their way to particular institutions of higher education are marked with particular complexity, it is fitting that the College Board, as a unique membership association of schools and colleges, attempts to assess the degree to which the system as a whole serves the needs of the parties involved.

We owe special gratitude to the individuals who agreed to take on the task and the challenge of studying various aspects of the "great sorting" and, through these monographs, to describe the intricacies and strengths of our system of college admission.

Donald M. Stewart
President
The College Board

Introduction

Admission to colleges and universities in the United States has increased tremendously during this century, especially since World War II. In addition to demographic changes—the explosion in enrollment of returning veterans, the "baby boom," and the increase of women and minorities participating in higher education—financial aid has also been a factor in the expanding higher education arena. Three entities joined forces in a financial aid partnership that assists students and families in their pursuit of the American dream.

A. *The Federal government*—through the GI Bill and Social Security; through Title IV of the Higher Education Amendments, especially with the rapid expansion of guaranteed loan programs.
B. *States*—through direct taxpayer subsidies to state-supported colleges and universities; through the growth of community college systems; and through state grant programs.
C. *Institutions*—through merit scholarships, need-based grants, payment plans, family loans, and tuition discounts.

Although students and their parents are expected to bear the primary responsibility for the cost of higher education, the expansion of programs and partners in the financial aid industry has shifted it from the "top right-hand drawer" of the admission director's desk to a multibillion-dollar juggling act in the center ring, involving thousands of financial aid professionals, appointed and elected public officials, academicians, and college counselors—and it affects the lives of millions of students.

As one might expect, this mammoth effort had to be anchored with guidelines to promote simplicity, equity, standardization, and accountability. Practices and policies, like budgets, often appear reasonable and appropriate in a "boom" or growth era. However, in a period of no growth or decline, the same practices and policies can be viewed as restrictive or inappropriate. This monograph will look at the evolution of financial aid as a function of higher education administration; evaluate past and current financial aid policies and practices and their impact on admission and enrollment; and recommend possible directions for meeting the challenges of the twenty-first century.

I have had the good fortune to know and work with many outstanding admission, enrollment management, and financial aid colleagues. Although I have borrowed and adapted ideas and drawn upon their experiences, any mistakes herein are mine. In particular, I want to thank John Maguire, my longstanding friend and associate in enrollment management for the past 20 years; Kathy Kurz, from the University of Rochester, with whom I've had the privilege of working for the past six years; and last and most important, Rhonda Norsetter, from the University of Wisconsin at Madison. More than anyone else, Rhonda has influenced my work and my writing through both her support and critical suggestions. She has constantly kept the theme persuasively and forcibly front and center—that in all we do, the student comes first.

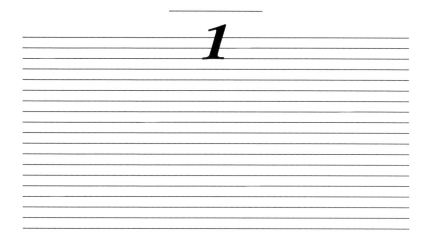

The Emergence of Financial Aid in U.S. Higher Education

**If I knew I was going to live this long, I'd have
taken better care of myself.**
Mickey Mantle

The History of Financial Aid

American higher education has evolved over the last century from
serving society's elite to espousing meritocratic ideals, to, most recently, a commitment to egalitarianism. As the goals and objectives
of postsecondary education expanded and society's concurrent demand for college graduates grew, student financial aid began to play

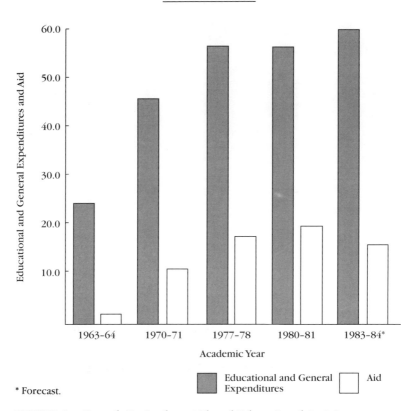

* Forecast.

Educational and General Expenditures □ Aid

FIGURE 1.   Growth In Student Aid and Educational Activity (Constant 1982 dollars in billions)

Source: Donald A. Gillespie and Nancy Carlson. *Trends in Student Aid: 1963 to 1983.* (Washington, D.C.: College Entrance Examination Board, 1983.)

an ever more important role in U.S. colleges and universities. (See Figure 1.) This explosion in higher education brought with it new participants, resources, and needs, all of which have contributed to the complex enterprise of financing higher education.

Federal Involvement

The federal government played an almost nonexistent role in the financing of higher education until after World War II. What government assistance existed was provided by the states. Most state funding was directed toward the land-grant, publicly subsidized institutions, with little or no involvement in the private sector. Private institutions granted occasional tuition remission awards to outstanding students, mostly academic scholarships, while periodically recognizing distinguished achievement on the athletic field or in the music chamber. For the most part, those who wanted to participate in the academy paid their own way, or more likely, had their parents pay their way. If a specific institution was too expensive, they found another at lower cost. They worked and saved until they had accumulated enough; many didn't go at all.

The so-called GI Bill, originally passed in the aftermath of World War II, was the federal government's largest categorical contribution to higher education until the late 1970s when it was supplanted by the federal Basic Educational Opportunity Grant (now called the Pell Grant) and Guaranteed Student Loan programs. The GI Bill and the programs that followed it changed the way the public looked at the responsibility for meeting educational costs. (See Table 1.) The idea of meritocracy was replaced by the goal of equal educational opportunity. The space race, President John F. Kennedy's "best and the brightest," and the Civil Rights movement all helped to speed up this process. Equal access and freedom of choice became the watchwords of the day as higher education was seen as the pathway to social and economic advancement. Congressmen, state legislators, and governors found themselves making policy with university presidents, college business officers, and education lobbyists. Historic sources of financial aid are summarized in Table 1. As the table indicates, to guarantee equal access and choice there had to be a redistribution and enlargement of student financial aid. Government monies, directed first at institutions for use at their discretion, and then as direct aid to students, became the vehicle used to meet this goal.

Why aid is important. Worthy as this goal is, the enrollment explosion of the 1960s and early 1970s left many institutions encumbered with a large debt service and increasingly significant fixed costs. This labor-intensive industry fell victim to the spiraling inflation of the 1970s. Given tripling energy costs and a stabilizing or shrinking college-bound population, tuition at many private institutions became prohibitive. In the 1980s, the federal government began to withdraw its commitment to the traditional student financial aid programs at U.S. colleges and universities. Total federal aid, including generally available aid in the Pell Grant and Guaranteed Student Loan programs,

TABLE 1. Aid Awarded to Postsecondary Students in Constant 1990 Dollars (in Millions), Selected Years 1963–64 to 1980–81

						Academic year						
	1963-64	1970-71	1971-72	1972-73	1973-74	1974-75	1975-76	1976-77	1977-78	1978-79	1979-80	1980-81
Federally supported programs												
Generally available aid												
Pell Grants	0	0	0	0	$ 140	$ 900	$ 2,207	$ 3,282	$ 3,314	$ 3,231	$ 4,218	$ 3,602
SEOG	0	$ 440	$ 487	$ 530	530	505	474	543	508	508	560	555
SSIG	0	0	0	0	0	48	46	97	125	121	129	109
CWS	0	748	762	811	830	745	695	971	979	932	1,003	996
Perkins Loans (NDSL)	$ 482	791	991	1,214	1,215	1,110	1,084	1,246	1,283	1,222	1,087	1,047
Income Contingent Loans	0	0	0	0	0	0	0	0	0	0	0	0
Guaranteed Loans	0	3,340	4,046	3,575	3,195	3,276	2,986	2,951	3,625	4,504	6,611	9,360
Subtotal	$ 482	$ 5,320	$ 6,285	$ 6,130	$ 5,910	$ 6,583	$ 7,493	$ 9,090	$ 9,834	$10,518	$13,609	$15,669
Specially directed aid												
Social Security	0	$ 1,642	$ 1,810	$ 2,140	$ 2,199	$ 2,256	$ 2,576	$ 2,784	$ 2,859	$ 2,819	$ 2,672	$ 2,842
Veterans	$ 284	3,689	4,192	5,911	6,342	8,462	9,852	6,674	5,635	4,152	3,067	2,587
Military	177	212	189	168	226	239	228	225	218	223	281	303
Other grants	37	52	63	83	94	145	148	149	172	187	192	184
Other loans	0	138	162	174	173	148	106	104	88	88	71	94
Subtotal	$ 498	$ 5,734	$ 6,416	$ 8,477	$ 9,034	$11,251	$12,911	$ 9,935	$ 8,972	$ 7,469	$ 6,283	$ 6,009
Total federal aid	$ 980	$11,054	$12,701	$14,607	$14,943	$17,834	$20,404	$19,024	$18,806	$17,987	$19,892	$21,678
State grant programs	237	777	854	962	1,021	1,065	1,155	1,354	1,413	1,385	1,327	1,209
Institutional and other grants	1,143	2,754	2,991	2,985	2,831	2,573	2,754	2,662	2,563	2,449	2,458	2,451
Total federal, state, and institutional aid	$2,360	$14,243	$16,123	$18,100	$18,358	$20,915	$23,642	$22,555	$22,351	$21,406	$23,148	$25,338

Source: *Trends in Student Aid: 1981–1991* (Washington, D.C.: College Entrance Examination Board, 1991).

as well as specially directed aid (Social Security, veterans' benefits, etc.), declined 3 percent in constant dollars. (See Table 2.) As states continued to subsidize the public sector (a policy driven by the goal of access), the tuition gap between public and private institutions widened.

The College Board estimated that in 1975-76 there was a $2-billion gap when the aggregate cost of attendance of full-time students was subtracted from parental contributions and financial aid from various sources. Today the estimates of that gap are as high as $10 billion. All the traditional partners—federal government, state government, institutions, and families—are under financial duress. Closing the gap will necessitate a radical restructuring of the partnership relationship and, most likely, seeking out new partners.

With the applicant pool shrinking and many fixed costs rising, postsecondary institutions today are struggling to maintain enrollment. Private higher education has used student aid as a resource for meeting enrollment goals, rather than as an instrument for implementing the worthy ideals of access and choice. Chester Finn, in his essay "Why Do We Need Financial Aid? or, Desanctifying Student Assistance," describes what has happened to colleges in a way viewed by many as overly pessimistic and cynical. He notes,

> The simplest way to state the difference—no doubt too simple a way—is that the higher education industry is fast losing the characteristics of a cartel and is becoming (some will say has already become) a collection of highly competitive vendors who do their utmost to attract purchasers, including furnishing an extraordinary array of price reductions, subsidies, special sales, rebates, and bargains. From a vendor's standpoint, student aid is just another term for these economic lures. From the purchaser's standpoint, it is becoming a mechanism for getting the best "deal." And from the perspective of the student aid provider, it is a way of achieving *his* or *her* purposes, whatever they may be, by intervening in the postsecondary marketplace. (1985, p. 15)

The vendor/customer analogy is not of course totally appropriate. (See Chapter 3.) However, given limited funds and an aggregate financial need far in excess of those monies, the distribution of student financial aid has become crucial, not only to the aspiring scholar-consumer of the goods and services, but also to institutions of higher learning that see it as strategic to their survival. Today more than $28 billion is spent in support of student financial assistance in postsecondary education.

TABLE 2. Aid Awarded to Postsecondary Students in Constant 1989 Dollars (in Millions)

Federally supported programs	1980-81	1981-82	1982-83	1983-84	1984-85	1985-86	1986-87	1987-88	Estimated 1988-89	Preliminary 1989-90	Percent Change '80-'81 to '89-'90
Generally available aid											
Pell Grants	$ 3,418	$ 3,030	$ 3,053	$ 3,401	$ 3,558	$ 4,066	$ 3,838	$ 4,001	$ 4,578	$ 4,370	28%
SEOG	527	476	433	440	438	467	446	449	433	432	−18%
SSIG	104	102	93	73	89	86	81	81	74	70	−32%
CWS	945	822	776	833	757	748	702	680	640	762	−19%
Perkins Loans (NDSL)	993	765	755	831	795	801	851	862	895	824	−17%
Income Contingent Loans	0	0	0	0	0	0	0	5	5	5	
Guaranteed loans	8,881	9,512	8,455	9,228	10,099	10,074	10,150	12,191	12,272	12,009	35%
(Stafford loans)	(8,878)	(9,422)	(8,204)	(8,843)	(9,553)	(9,492)	(9,289)	(9,765)	(9,542)	(9,431)	6%
(SLS)	(0)	(19)	(100)	(180)	(260)	(306)	(580)	(1,959)	(2,063)	(1,795)	
(PLUS)	(3)	(71)	(150)	(204)	(285)	(276)	(281)	(467)	(666)	(783)	
Subtotal	$14,868	$14,707	$13,565	$14,805	$15,736	$16,242	$16,067	$18,268	$18,896	$18,473	24%
Specially directed aid											
Social Security	$ 2,696	$ 2,630	$ 926	268	$ 41	0	0	0	0	0	−100%
Veterans	2,455	1,780	1,712	1,398	1,178	984	873	816	741	$ 586	−76%
Military	287	306	336	362	386	390	402	374	340	357	24%
Other grants	174	139	108	75	71	77	82	99	104	109	−37%
Other loans	89	143	265	339	383	425	352	319	340	341	283%
Subtotal	$ 5,701	$ 4,998	$ 3,346	$ 2,442	$ 2,059	$ 1,876	$ 1,710	$ 1,608	$ 1,528	$ 1,394	−76%
Total federal aid	$20,569	$19,705	$16,911	$17,248	$17,795	$18,118	$17,777	$19,876	$20,425	$19,867	−3%
State grant programs	1,147	1,213	1,270	1,347	1,434	1,494	1,597	1,610	1,618	1,742	52%
Institutionally awarded aid	2,950	2,961	3,165	3,509	3,778	4,188	4,799	5,069	5,332	5,593	90%
Total federal, state, and institutional aid	$24,665	$23,879	$21,347	$22,104	$23,007	$23,799	$24,174	$26,555	$27,375	$27,202	0%

Source: *Trends in Student Aid: 1981–1991* (Washington, D.C.: College Entrance Examination Board, 1991).

The structure of postsecondary education has also changed with the addition of proprietary institutions. (These schools, unlike public and private colleges and universities, are operated on a for-profit basis and most of them provide vocational training of some sort.) These newcomers exploded on the postsecondary scene in the 1980s and now capture, for example, more than a quarter of the Pell Grant funds authorized annually. (See Table 3.) New players have also come on the scene in the financial aid arena because it, too, is viewed as an industry where money can be made. These include financial institutions providing loans to students, and consultants and scholarship research services that help students identify sources of financial aid for a fee. Not all of these new players have had the public's or the students' best interests in mind.

The History of Need Analysis

But this basically simple idea (need) has become enormously complex since those dispensing aid, whether government officials or college scholarship officers, naturally want a uniform and equitable basis for assessing the need of different students. It will not do to simply ask the individual or his parents how much they are prepared to pay. (Finn 1978, p. 54)

As briefly alluded to earlier, financial aid in its earliest incarnation was awarded on the basis of merit—whether academic, athletic, or artistic. However, as college costs increased, the concept of need-based financial aid assumed greater importance. In essence, need-based aid provides the difference between what a student (and his or her parents) can pay and the cost of attending a given institution.

Needless to say, determining need became a principal focus. Harvard and Yale began to look at the question of need in the early 1950s. Under the leadership of Dean John Munro, Harvard developed the first need analysis formula and presented it in 1953 (Staple 1979). Income and assets were examined in relation to a family's ability to pay, which was determined by researching what families at different incomes or levels had been providing for their child's education over a number of years. Simply put, Munro "taxed" net income between 8 percent and 12 percent based on family size. The system employed to determine need today, after almost 40 years of gyrations and manipulations, is not much different, at least in terms of philosophy and

TABLE 3.   Student Aid Distribution, 1986-87

	Public	*Private nonprofit*	*Proprietary*
Percentage of students receiving any aid	38.0%	65.3%	84.0%
Percentage of students receiving federal aid	28.5%	48.4%	80.6%
Percentage of students receiving state aid	12.5%	25.4%	10.3%
Percentage of students receiving institution-based aid	8.8%	39.0%	4.1%
Percentage of students receiving other aid	6.0%	11.2%	3.7%
Average student charges* (gross of student aid)	$3,805	$9,676	$5,198
Average aid amount for aided students	$2,887	$5,633	$4,025

* Includes tuition and fees plus room and board.
Note: Some students receive aid from more than one source.
Source: Michael McPherson and Morton Schapiro, *Keeping College Affordable: Government's Role in Promoting Educational Opportunity* (Washington, D.C.: 1991).

approach, the philosophy being that parents have primary responsibility in financing their children's education, the approach being a progressive assessment on a family's discretionary income, thereby permitting institutions to provide financial assistance for low-income students.

A Standardized Procedure

The federal government provided motivation for colleges and universities to employ a standardized procedure for determining need when, in 1964 and 1965, the College Work-Study (CWS) and Educational Opportunity Grant (EOG) programs were created under the Higher Education Amendments. Both programs were contingent on family income. Differing methods for analyzing need ultimately evolved into the Uniform Methodology in 1974, the work of the National Task Force on Student Aid Problems, chaired by Francis

Keppel, former United States Commissioner of Education. The task force made additional recommendations, including an equity approach to financial aid "packaging" (i.e., determining the mix of loans, scholarships/grants, work-study, and family contributions best suited to finance a given student's education). (See Chapter 5.) The task force was followed by the National Coalition for Coordination of Student Financial Aid, which conducted an annual review of the Uniform Methodology and recommended any changes or modifications to it. The coalition also identified the core information needed to award federally provided grant monies.

The method used to analyze financial need became a federal law under the Higher Education Amendments passed by Congress in 1986. This Congressional Methodology became effective in the 1988-89 academic year. The mandate included a master calendar for developing the forms used to apply for financial aid, need analysis updates, and a provision that all changes to the methodology must be approved by Congress. Finally, this law called for the formation of an independent advisory committee on student financial assistance with the specific function of providing technical expertise with regard to need analysis. The Congressional Methodology today serves as the national standard in determining what a family is expected to contribute, and does not consider academic ability, character, or other criteria that an institution might employ in the selection of aid recipients. Sweeping changes to the Higher Education Amendments have been proposed under the 1991-92 reauthorization that would affect need analysis, the delivery system, and the Pell Grant Program, as well as introduce a "direct-lending" pilot.

A Question of Judgment

Federal guidelines notwithstanding, the judgment of the financial aid administrator has been and continues to be indispensable in awarding assistance to students. Financial aid professionals have an ever-increasing share of center stage in higher education. As the number of students decreases, as institutions seek the most qualified, and as resources lose their purchasing power in relation to rising education costs, the financial aid officer finds herself or himself in the precarious position of trying to serve three masters—the government, the institution, and the student. Few positions in higher education are as fraught with potential conflict and, at the same time, are of as much significance to the survival of the institution and the lives of students and their families.

Access and Choice

In his essay "Financial Aid and Student Persistence," Alexander Astin (1975) identifies six purposes of student financial aid:

1. To provide greater access to higher education
2. To ensure that students complete their studies (persistence)
3. To provide incentives to perform well academically
4. To reward merit
5. To influence student choice
6. To redistribute wealth

Purposes 1 and 5 are the cornerstones upon which the financial aid profession has been built. In fact, student aid forged the way to today's egalitarian concept of universal access to postsecondary education. At the heart of this goal, however, is the novel idea that financial assistance should be based on need rather than merit. Finn's (1978) landmark "Scholars, Dollars, and Bureaucrats" describes need-based financial aid as serving a dual purpose: (1) bringing college within the reach of people who might not otherwise be willing or able to enroll and (2) bringing students to colleges that might not otherwise have enough students or, at the very least, enough students of the sort they favor.

"Access" and "choice" became the watchwords of the 1970s, in response to both the population boom and the Civil Rights movement—fortified by new federal legislation. Although some have argued that aid has not been effective, Larry Leslie and Paul Brinkman, in *The Economic Value of Higher Education* (1988), document the impact of student financial aid through three methods of evaluation: (1) an econometric analysis of enrollment behavior; (2) student opinion survey; and (3) calculation of higher education participation rates. Regarding access, they show through an econometric analysis that "without aid, mostly in the form of nonrepayable grants, the enrollment of low-income students would be reduced by 20–40 percent

. . . middle-income student enrollment lessened by 7.4–19.5 percent . . . and high-income student enrollment lessened by 2.5–3.5 percent." These authors argue that low-income, low-ability students are most responsive to aid, while high-income, high-ability students are less responsive. Finally, they conclude that in 1982-83, the enrollment of between 1 and 1.3 million full-time students was dependent on grant aid. McPherson and Schapiro, in the Brookings Institution publication *Keeping College Affordable* (1991), make additional convincing arguments.

Choice

Choice, on the other hand, is more difficult to evaluate. A good deal of attention has been focused on groups that have not traditionally participated in higher education, to see whether financial aid has encouraged their participation. In the mid 1970s many, including Leslie and Weathersby, were uncertain about the relationship between financial aid and student choice. "Two-thirds [of high school seniors] apply to only one institution. And 91 percent of those that apply to more than one institution go to the institution of their first choice" (Weathersby 1976). In terms of the almost four in five U.S. under-graduates who go to publicly subsidized colleges and universities, this is of course true in the aggregate. However, it is not true of private, competitive schools or of flagship public institutions which are perceived as equal to or just a notch below the Ivy League. Leslie and Brinkman take the opposing point of view, that student aid does influence student choice, although they state that

> the impact of student aid on choice is difficult to analyze perhaps more so than its impact on access. The process of choosing an institution is complex. There are several points in the process when student aid, or the likelihood thereof, could be influential. For in-stance, general notions about the availability of aid would be im-portant at the time when students and their families initially think about the range of attendance possibilities. (1988, p. 171)

However, they further state, "Student aid is an effective way of chang-ing net-pricing differentials among competing institutions. . . . An institution can increase its enrollment share by increasing the aid it offers, other things staying the same" (1988, p. 171). And finally, Leslie and Brinkman report,

[It] may be that aid has worked well enough to maintain the distribution of students, more or less, while helping to strengthen the financial position of the institutions. The enrollment share of private institutions is essentially unchanged since the early 1970s, when the rapid growth in aid began after precipitous declines in the 1950s and 1960s. (1988, p. 172)

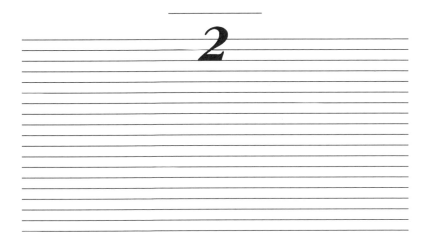

The Evolution of Financial Aid Policies and Practices

**All right, everyone, line up alphabetically
according to your height.**
Casey Stengel

The financial aid officer is constantly struggling with trade-off decisions in the distribution of aid. These trade-offs typically involve such issues as access versus choice, individual needs versus institutional needs, and the financial need of the student versus his or her merit. The values that guide the financial aid officer in making these decisions are stated in a series of principles and practices, some of which are quoted below to provide a point of reference for further discussion in this text. (Numbers refer to the order in which they are published in the *Manual for Student Aid Administrators.*)

Principles:

1. The purpose of any financial aid program—institutional, governmental, or private—should be to provide monetary assistance to students who can benefit from further education but who cannot do so without such assistance. The primary purpose of a collegiate financial aid program should be to provide financial assistance to accepted students who, without such aid, would be unable to attend that college.

5. Financial aid should be offered only after determination that the resources of the family are insufficient to meet the student's educational expenses. The amount of aid offered should not exceed the amount needed to meet the difference between the student's total educational expenses and the family's resources.

6. The amount and type of self-help expected from students should be related to the circumstances of the individual. In the assignment of funds to those students designated to receive financial aid, the largest amounts of total grant assistance should go to students with the least ability to pay.

10. Concern for the student should be paramount. Financial aid should be administered in such a manner that other interests, important though they may be, are subordinate to the needs of students.

Practices:

Organization and administration. Establish administrative procedures that are responsive to the needs of students as well as to the needs of institutions by:

5. Conducting surveys to assist in the development of realistic student budgets.

6. Utilizing a recognized standard need analysis system consistently to determine the ability of students and their families to pay for educational costs.

7. Considering the student's individual circumstances when offering self-help aid and determining self-help expectation.

8. Using all forms of aid—grant, loan, employment—and considering other resources available to the student in order to provide the most equitable apportionment of limited funds to eligible students.

9. Meeting the full need of students to the extent possible within the institution's capabilities.

11. Providing students who are not offered financial aid with the specific reason(s) for the denial of aid and, to the extent possible, assisting them in finding alternative sources of aid.

15. Considering the inclusion of students, faculty members, and administrators on institutional committees that are responsible for establishing financial aid policies.

16. Coordinating the administration of financial aid through a central office to ensure consistency in making awards to students and the most efficient use of available funds.

17. Notifying students of financial aid decisions as early as possible in order to serve students' best interests and when possible coordinating these notifications with those of admissions decisions.

18. Sharing information with other institutions and agencies about mutual aid candidates to ensure comparable financial aid awards, thereby permitting a student freedom in choosing an institution.

Research and professional development. Continue to contribute to the evaluation and progress of the profession of student financial aid administration by:

19. Developing and conducting research programs that will contribute to the solution of problems and advancement of knowledge in the field of financial aid.

20. Conducting periodic reviews of the institution's total financial aid process in order to serve students and the institution better.

21. Encouraging the continued professional development of financial aid administrators by providing opportunities to join and participate in professional aid administrators' associations and organizations dedicated to the advancement of sound principles and practices and the extension of knowledge in student financial aid administration. (College Entrance Examination Board 1991, pp. 1.1–1.2)

These are laudatory and even lofty "rules of the trade." However, the financial aid administrator is routinely confronted by student, family, institutional, legal, and even regulatory conflicts with these guidelines in the normal performance of her or his duties. Two examples of these follow:

a. Congressional Methodology assumes that the family contribution to meet educational costs will be derived in large part from current income. Table 4 displays the parents' contribution (PC) calculated on a monthly basis according to four different financing scenarios. Some would argue that at the low-income level (below $20,000 a year) the expected contribution is reasonable. On the other hand, to expect a family, perhaps a two-earner household with a total income of $60,000, to take $9,500 out of its after-tax income (that is, more than 20 percent of net income) is viewed by many as too harsh an assessment. Although the value of saving and borrowing is clearly demonstrated in this chart, the current need analysis system has not encouraged American families to save. In fact, there exists a belief among many families that savings may reduce the chances of receiving financial aid. The aid officer is thus forced to discern the extent of a family's commitment to meet educational costs—that is, ability, necessity, and reality. Establishing the family's true situation and responding in both the student's and the institution's best interest, within the regulations, is always a challenge. Appropriate responses are often very hard to come by and frequently require a case-by-case interpretation.

b. Financial aid professionals are currently wrestling with issues having to do with integrity, simplicity, and an imbalance between loans and grants, which were major themes as Congress debated the reauthorization of the Higher Education Amendments during the 1991 and 1992 sessions. *Integrity* for the most part focuses on the area of loan default. Here there are real differences among the various sectors of higher education that affect aid practices. *Simplicity* is reflected in the attempt to find vehicles and instruments that will encourage access to the aid process while, at the same time, guaranteeing that sufficient data are collected to make a fair and equitable judgment of a family's ability to pay. Again there exists the potential for tension between professional guidelines and regulatory processes. The *loan–grant imbalance* can best be demonstrated by examination of Figure 2. Note that grants declined from 66 percent in 1970–71 to 48 percent in 1983–84. Today they comprise less than 40 percent of generally available federal student aid. Loans, on the other hand, increased from 29 percent in 1970–71 to 48 percent in 1983–84. Today, they represent over 60 percent of generally available federal student aid. The financial aid officer constantly tries to juggle sources of aid consistent with the rules of the trade and available resources.

TABLE 4. Parents' Contribution (PC) Calculated on a Monthly Basis According to Four Different Financing Scenarios

Annual family income	Expected parents' contribution for one year	Pay out of current income alone; monthly payments for 4 years of enrollment	Borrow-in-full; monthly repayments for 4 years of and 10 years after enrollment	Borrow-and-save; monthly cost to save and borrow for 4 years before, during, and after enrollment	Save-in-full; monthly savings for 8 years before and 4 years during enrollment
$20,000	$ 220	$ 18	$ 7	$ 7	$ 5
30,000	1,740	145	53	48	43
40,000	3,700	310	113	100	90
50,000	6,510	542	200	179	158
60,000	9,500	790	290	260	235
70,000	12,510	1,044	385	338	309
80,000	15,520	1,293	480	420	380
90,000	18,530	1,545	570	503	450

Note: The figures represent parents' contributions—from income only—for 1991-92; assume the older parent, age 45, employed; the other parent is not employed; income only from employment; no unusual circumstances; standard deductions on U.S. income tax; one undergraduate family member in college; and family size of four.

Source: *Manual for Student Aid Administrators* (New York: College Entrance Examination Board, 1991).

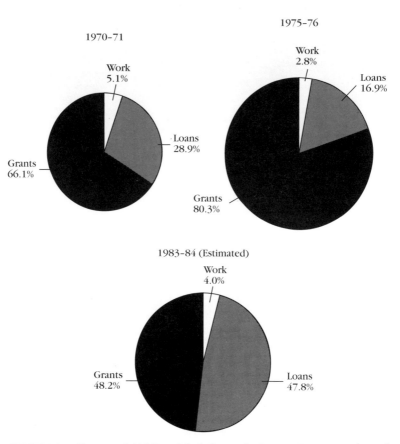

FIGURE 2. Shares of Aid Provided through Grants, Loans, and Work (Current and constant 1982 dollars in millions)

Note: Figures are scaled to total aid in 1982 dollars.
Source: Donald A. Gillespie and Nancy Carlson, *Trends in Student Aid: 1963–1983* (Washington, D.C.: College Entrance Examination Board, 1983).

Conclusion

In the current competitive marketplace, some of the principles, practices, and policies that implement them are on a collision course with institutional needs, priorities, goals, and possibly even survival. Does that mean the financial aid profession has or should abandon its principles and practices? The premise of this monograph is *absolutely not*! However, unilateral adherence to all principles and practices at every type of institution in every sector, two-year and four-year, public and private, is not realistic given the changing needs of society. Financial aid principles and practices, and the policies instituted to implement them, must be informed by values, not driven by the market. Discussion of and agreement on these values must extend well beyond the walls of the financial aid office. But the financial aid office is likely to continue playing a key role in the balancing act between student, government, institutional, and societal needs. Subsequent chapters will examine trends that influence these institutional needs, the differences between the sectors in our dual system, and the financial aid strategies that have been devised to meet institutional admission and enrollment goals and objectives.

Institutional Need for Financial Aid

It gets late early out there.
Yogi Berra

Higher Education, The American Dream

According to *Money Magazine* in fall of 1990, next to catastrophic illness and environmental problems, families rate the cost of education as the third most significant obstacle to the fulfillment of the American Dream. Concern over the cost of education was tied with war in the responses of most families, even though the poll was taken when the Persian Gulf crisis dominated the news.

As noted earlier, the 1960s and 1970s saw a tremendous growth in the number of students enrolled in higher education. (See Table 5.) Yet since that explosion, participation *rates* have not really con-

TABLE 5. Fall Enrollment of Full-Time-Equivalent Students (Thousands)

	Undergraduate	*Total*
1983	7,900 (projection)	9,055 (projection)
1982	8,043 (estimate)	9,092
1981	7,970 (estimate)	9,015
1980	7,697	8,749
1979	7,460	8,487
1977	7,398	8,415
1975	7,493	8,481
1970	5,976	6,737
1963	(not available)	3,696

Source: Donald A. Gillespie and Nancy Carlson, *Trends in Student Aid: 1963 to 1983* (Washington, D.C.: College Entrance Examination Board, 1983).

tinued to grow in spite of the fact that more funds have been pumped into the system. As Table 6 indicates, this has to do with the rapid growth in costs of attendance.

Relationship of Aid and Costs

These cost increases have led to heavy criticism of higher education, most notably from former Secretary of Education William Bennett, who castigated colleges and universities in this country for being "greedy." Bennett wrote, in a background paper circulated to state governors and the Department of Education (and quoted in the *New York Times*, February 18, 1987, Op Ed page), "Federal student aid is also important in allowing colleges to raise their costs because it constitutes a major subsidy of higher education that insulates them from normal market forces of supply and demand." The paper later states, "the federal government now provides a subsidy of about $15 billion per year to the higher education industry. It is hard to believe that a $15-billion subsidy of any industry would have no effect on pricing."

In 1987, William Bowen, then president of Princeton, wrote a white paper, "The Student Aid/Tuition Nexus," in response to the Bennett charge. In reviewing Bennett's argument, Bowen questioned certain economic assumptions made by Bennett:

TABLE 6. Cost of Attendance and Income 1980–81 to 1989–90 (Constant 1989 Dollars)

| | Cost of Attendance | | | | | Income | |
	Private university	Private four-year	Public university	Public four-year	Public two-year	Personal (per capita)	Median family
1980–81	$ 9,407	$ 7,516	$3,882	$3,468	$2,902	$12,677	$31,637
1981–82	9,808	7,837	4,057	3,563	2,929	12,605	30,540
1982–83	10,780	8,392	4,297	3,829	3,018	12,491	30,111
1983–84	11,337	8,824	4,419	4,001	3,087	12,886	30,719
1984–85	12,016	9,208	4,574	4,127	3,293	13,435	31,547
1985–86	12,576	9,746	4,725	4,145	3,397	13,684	31,992
1986–87	13,691	10,344	4,985	4,339	3,332	14,133	33,328
1987–88	14,000	10,552	4,945	4,551	3,283	14,348	33,805
1988–89	14,410	10,874	5,022	4,633	3,259	14,789	33,742
1989–90 (est.)	15,002	11,437	5,435	4,853	3,414	14,961	NA
% Change 1980–81 to 1989–90	59.5%	52.2%	40.0%	39.9%	17.6%	18.0%	

Notes: Cost of attendance includes tuition, fees, and room and board costs. Beginning in 1986–87 board data are based on 20 meals per week, rather than on meals served 7 days a week. Since some institutions do not serve three meals per day, the newer board rates are higher but reflect a more accurate accounting of total board costs. 1989–90 are preliminary data. Note that these averages apply to *undergraduate* costs only; and are weighted by enrollment to reflect average cost to the student rather than the average charge by institutions.

Income data are for the calendar year in which the academic year begins.

NA = Not available.

Source: Lawrence Gladieux and Janet Hansen, *Trends in Student Aid 1980 to 1990* (Washington, D.C.: College Entrance Examination Board, 1990).

1. The firms in the industry are profit maximizers and would have no interest in, and no reason for, holding the price below its profit-maximizing level.

2. In a perfectly functioning market that involves profit-maximizing firms, the market will always clear—that is, there could never be persistent excess demand, without unsatisfied customers still clamoring for "the product" at the stated price, since any (temporary) excess demand would drive up the price until the excess demand was eliminated.

3. The firms have no particular interest in who buys their product—a customer is a customer as long as the bills are paid. The composition of the clientele is otherwise irrelevant.

Bowen argues that Bennett's interpretation would apply only in a very rough sense to the profit-making, proprietary sector of higher education. But this sector is clearly not at the center of the debate and it is important, Bowen states, to ask directly whether the Bennett model fits at all with the realities of the other sectors of higher education—including the private research universities and selective colleges that tend to be the price setters and are the particular targets of the secretary. Bowen argues that the Bennett model is inappropriate for these institutions and, in fact, the relationship between student aid funds and tuition is precisely the opposite of that described by the secretary. Specifically, Bowen notes:

1. The research universities and selective colleges are not profit maximizers. The budget-making process in these institutions will involve students, faculty members, and administrative staff, as well as trustees, and those involved institutional agents assign a significant weight to the objective of keeping rates of increase in tuition as low as they can possibly be, consistent with the need to offer education of high quality to an appropriately qualified and constituted student population. These institutions care greatly about the all-too-real burdens imposed on their students and parents by the tuition the institutions feel they must charge. Conscious, conscientious efforts are made to moderate rates of increase in tuition.

2. The tuition charged does not come close to "clearing the market." One of the most evident results of this budgeting process, as it is revealed each year to large numbers of disappointed applicants for admission, is that there is a substantial excess demand for places in each entering class.

3. Colleges and universities care intensely about who "consumes their product." A major goal of these institutions is to enable the ablest of students, from a wide variety of backgrounds, to attend, whatever their financial circumstances. (1987, pp. 3–4)

Bowen clearly differentiates between corporations, such as McDonald's, J. C. Penney, and General Motors, and higher education institutions. There is abundant additional evidence that the Bennett model is wrong. For example:

1. Only half of the students enrolled in higher education receive financial aid. And many of those who do get it receive so little aid that its impact on behavior is minimal. Therefore, federal aid insulates fewer than half of the enrolled students from the impact of increased costs.

2. The pattern of funding of student aid runs counter to what would be expected in the Bennett scenario. The increases in federal aid were greatest in the 1970s when increases in college costs lagged behind inflation. In the 1980s, federal aid was down and tuitions were up.

3. Tuition increases do not have as great an impact on eligibility for federal aid as Bennett assumes. A 10 percent change in charges would equal about a 1 percent change in Pell Grant eligibility. A 10 percent increase in charges produces about a 5 percent change in Guaranteed Student Loan eligibility. And a 10 percent increase in charges would produce no increase in eligibility for campus-based programs, such as College Work-Study. Thus, a 10 percent increase in charges produces at the very most a 2 percent increase in federal aid eligibility.

In addition, despite the public perception that tuition increases are a recent phenomenon, higher education costs have been growing at a rate faster than the Consumer Price Index since the turn of the century (with the exception of the period during the two major wars and the Great Depression). (See Figure 3.) Nonetheless, the damage was done and the U.S. public's faith in higher education was severely shaken.

Although the Bennett argument was wrongheaded, a relationship does exist between the tuition charged and the need for student aid, which raises another problem for the financial aid officer as well as the admission officer. It is widely assumed that, if tuition increases approximately x percent, student aid needs to increase only x percent

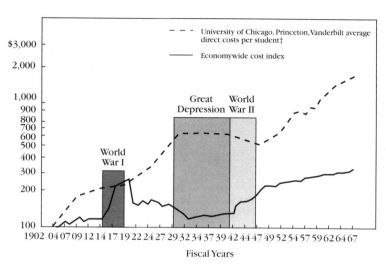

FIGURE 3. Direct Costs Per Student, Compared with an Economywide Cost Index*

* Index, 1904-05 = 100
† Chosen as a representative group of private universities
Source: William G. Bowen, *The Economics of the Major Private Universities* (Berkeley: Carnegie Commission, 1968).

to keep pace. Two hypothetical scenarios follow: one describes this relationship as it might logically be construed and the other relationship as it actually exists.

Effect on Students

Any review of enrollment-related trends and financial aid would be incomplete without mention of student retention. To be sure, increased attention has been paid in the last decade to retention or persistence of students, particularly as it pertains to financial aid policies and practices. Leslie and Brinkman (1988) note,

> One, the overall effect is to permit aid recipients to persist about as well as nonrecipients. Two, the effect differs along several dimensions, the most important of which would seem to be that (a) the size of the effect has grown in a positive direction in recent years; (b) nonwhite aid recipients do not persist as well as white

aid recipients; (c) persistence is enhanced by larger amounts of aid; and (d) when aid forms are compared to one another, grant and scholarship aid have a more positive effect on persistence than do loans. (p. 179)

Of late there have been a number of rules and regulations introduced such as satisfactory academic progress and ability to benefit, which impact upon aid eligibility, particularly of less well qualified students who typically are among those in greatest financial need.

When these trends are joined with declining demographics, a more sophisticated consumer, a growing gap between public- and private-sector tuitions, the end result is a "buyer's" rather than a "seller's" market. At many institutions, financial aid has become a strategic institutional response to these developments.

The "Needy" Middle Class

Finally, to further add to this already complex dynamic, the 1970s saw new players arrive on U.S. campuses needing financial assistance—students from middle- and even upper-income families. The

The Relationship Between Cost and Scholarship/Grant Increases.

Scenario I

Charges currently set at $15,000 for tuition, fees, room and board. (Additional costs for books, personal expenses, and travel not included.) Number of undergraduates currently receiving financial support from the university is 2,350 at $4,550 each for a total of $10,700,000.
Assume a 7 percent increase in charges—$1,050 increase per student. Assume this increase is met in the following manner for the average student:

1.	Additional parental contribution (current contribution of $4,100 × 6% inflation) =	$	250
2.	Additional governmental support (current support of $2,000 × 6% inflation) =	$	120
3.	Additional self-help (current loan and work of $3,500 × 7% increase) =	$	250
4.	Additional university scholarship support =	$	430

Total new resources to meet cost increase = $ 1,050
Increase in scholarship/grant needed =
    $430 × 2,350 students = $1,010,500
Thus a 7 percent increase in charges would require a 9.4 percent increase in the scholarship/grant budget.

The Relationship Between Cost and Scholarship/Grant Increases.

Scenario II

Charges currently set at $15,000 for tuition, fees, room and board. (Additional costs for books, personal expenses, and travel not included.) Number of undergraduates currently receiving financial support from the university is 2,350 at $4,550 each for a total of $10,700,000.

Assume a 7 percent increase in charges—$1,050 increase per student. Assume this increase is met in the following manner for the average student:

1.	Additional parental contribution =	$	0
2.	Additional governmental support =	$	0
3.	Additional self-help =	$	0
4.	Additional university scholarship/grant support =	$	1,050

Total new resources to meet cost increase = $ 1,050

Increase in scholarship/grant needed =

    $1,050 × 2,350 students = $2,467,500

Thus a more realistic outcome would find a 7 percent increase in charges produced a 23 percent increase in this scholarship/grant budget. This latter scenario was the most common at private institutions in the 1980s.

rapid increase in college costs made families with $30- to $70-thousand incomes, and some with even higher incomes and several children in college, eligible for financial assistance. Consequently, although federal and state programs were initially geared toward low-income students, in the late 1970s and 1980s, scholarship budgets grew at colleges and universities, not because of increases in enrollment, but rather because of an emerging need for financial assistance among middle-class families.

In search of a public policy to respond to this growing financial need, the idea of tuition tax credits was introduced in 1977. In response, Congress adopted the Middle Income Student Assistance Act (MISAA), and for a brief period of time, from 1978–81, Guaranteed Student Loans and Pell Grants were available to this population. It is important to note that while the effect may have relieved institutions of the responsibility for meeting this emerging financial need of the middle class, the expanding eligibility for the Pell Grant program had the effect of reducing college attendance rates among students from low-income families. In 1981, the Reagan administration began to withdraw this recently introduced support, and once again, the responsibility for meeting the new, growing need of students fell on

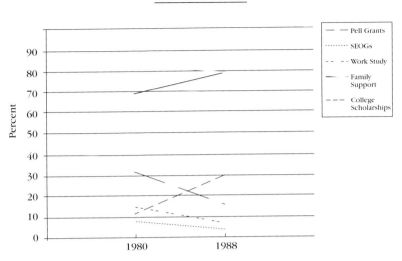

FIGURE 4. Percentage of College Freshmen Receiving Various Types of Financial Aid

institutions and families. (See Figure 4.) Although financial aid budgets doubled and sometimes tripled during the 1980s, many high-cost institutions experienced the phenomenon of "middle-class melt." Private institutions saw enrollments stay constant or grow at the low-income and high-income ends of the continuum, while students from middle-income families declined as a percentage of the student body. The extent of this melt, however, has been debated (Spies 1990; Schapiro et al. 1990). Nonetheless, the fact remains that U.S. colleges and universities are today serving a much broader income range of needy students than ever before.

Recruitment and Financial Aid

Enrollment Management

The foregoing suggests that the financial aid situation may be militating against student enrollment across the socioeconomic spectrum. Yet, at the same time, many colleges and universities are actively seeking students to fill their classes. The response has been a variety of recruitment and retention strategies that often fall under the rubric of "enrollment management." In an article entitled "To the Organized

Go the Students," John Maguire (1976) defined enrollment management as "a process that brings together often disparate functions having to do with recruiting, funding, tracking, retaining, and replacing students as they move toward, within, and away from our institutions." There are any number of models of this concept today in American colleges and universities. Organizationally, they tend to be headed either by a chief enrollment officer or by a committee representing a variety of functions, from administrative to academic, from student affairs to finance. Chief enrollment officers, with such titles as dean or even vice president, have assumed increasingly more visible positions in the institutional hierarchy. As with organization, there tends to be a wide array of enrollment management goals and objectives linked to institutionally specific issues and challenges. Two of the goals, again quoting Maguire, are

> *admissions marketing*—to develop an admissions marketing program in order to attract outstanding students in sufficient numbers during a period of national enrollment declines, and *pricing and financial aid strategies*—to implement pricing and financial aid strategies that will optimize the institution's ability to attract and retain the desired academic, racial/ethnic, and socioeconomic mix of students. (p. 17)

As will be described in the next chapter, enrollment management is organizationally more prevalent in private institutions than in public, although it is present in both. State budgets are being squeezed. The demand for public dollars has increased from all areas of society— elementary and secondary education, welfare, health, unemployment, social security, etc. Additionally, in the 1980s, the Reagan administration pushed much of the financial support for domestic concerns onto state budgets. As a consequence, public institutions are finding it increasingly more important to coordinate all aspects of their enrollment functions for efficiency, as well as to maximize the institution's ability to meet the goal of access which itself has been the cornerstone of public higher education. Thus many public institutions also have turned to enrollment management, but for different reasons than private institutions.

Effect on Financial Aid

The enrollment management concept presents admission officers with a new set of concerns, since it deals with student enrollment as a whole, not just new students. Thus, the focus is not only on the recruitment, admission, and enrollment of new students, but also on the retention of these new students (freshman and transfer), that is, student persistence through graduation. Financial aid officers typically have been more sensitive toward retention but most recently have made the direct link between their policies and practices and an institution's ability to achieve comprehensive enrollment goals. Of course, it seems obvious and logical that attention needs to be paid to the whole rather than just part. Yet, before the enrollment management concept was introduced, many institutions ran freshman financial aid offices under a different set of policies and practices, and with different goals and objectives, than the "university" or "college" aid office. These dual policies and practices were likely to favor the continuing student population over the new student population. And, in fact, because of the lack of coordination between offices (sometimes with entirely different reporting lines—admission reporting to an academic or student affairs vice president and financial aid to a finance vice president), the institution could be unaware that some of its policies and practices militated against meeting its new student objectives. For example, in the 1960s and 1970s, some institutional aid budgets were routinely divided by four, and one quarter was handed to the freshman financial aid office to enroll the new class. This practice entirely missed the point that an admission office typically does not enroll a quarter of the enrollment in any given year but more likely a third and sometimes, at institutions with low retention rates, half of the student body.

This type of allocation puts the admission office at a disadvantage in its ability to enroll the freshman class, often requiring that more students be accepted than could be accommodated because fewer would accept admission offers due to the lack of institutional financial aid. Ironically, less qualified students so accepted, upon completion of their freshman year, would then fall under the jurisdiction of the "university" or "college" aid office and be given more favorable treatment because proportionately more money would be available to support continuing students than was available at the time of entry. Formal links created under an enrollment management structure reduced the frequency of these inconsistencies.

Our Dual System
of Higher Education:
Sector Differences and
Sector Similarities

**The secret of managing is to keep the guys who hate you
away from the guys who are undecided.**
Casey Stengel

Increased competition for students and radically different approaches
to funding pitted public and private institutions against each other so
dramatically that the higher education lobby was virtually ineffective
during the 1972 and 1976 reauthorizations of the Higher Education
Amendments.

Sector differences are most apparent in the areas of mission, size, financial aid funding sources, clientele, and type of financial aid available. (See Table 7.) Similarities are most frequently found in terms of organizational structure and in the way in which aid is targeted to specific populations. Public institutions are often part of "multicampus systems" that share a name, core curriculum, transferability of credits, and, often, fee structures. Private colleges and universities on occasion have satellite campuses but are not "systems" per se. Public institutions are often, although not always, land grant (the institution has the mission of serving all state residents). These differences have profound implications for admission as well as for financial aid practices. For example, in public institutions, aid would only be targeted to populations whose participation was judged to be conducive to the public good, e.g., low-income or otherwise disadvantaged students. In the public sector, the vast majority of available funds to support student educational costs are received from federal and state governments; typically, somewhere between 80 and 90 percent of all student aid at public institutions comes from those two sources. At many independent institutions, far less than half comes from federal and state governments.

There are similarities, however, in the way both sectors try to advance equal education opportunity. It is far from uncommon to find targeted aid and minimal or no "self-help" components (whereby the student provides his or her own monies through working, loans, or parental assistance) in financial aid packages directed at low-income students and at minority students in both the public and private sectors. This strategy is generally accepted as being in the public good, thereby allowing state funds to flow to target populations. At public institutions, financial aid officers would cite access as their primary goal; this is a function of the land-grant mission of these institutions. Both admission and financial aid policies and practices enable students to attend, regardless of financial circumstances. Public institutions, therefore, are less likely to differentiate according to the demonstrated academic ability of an applicant. (When awarding financial aid, gift aid targeted for high-ability students, received by the institution from a foundation set up for this purpose, is a typical exception to this practice.) The financial aid officer at a public institution views her or his job as doing the best to meet the admitted student's financial need, whatever it may be. This, however, only

TABLE 7. Revenues of Public and Private Colleges and Universities (percentage of total)

Academic year	Public Institutions					Private Institutions				
	Gross tuition	Governments*		Gifts and endowment earnings	Other	Gross tuition	Governments*		Gifts and endowment earnings	Other
		Federal	State and local				Federal	State and local		
1939–40	0.20%	0.13%	0.61%	0.04%	0.01%	0.55%	0.01%	0.03%	0.38%	0.03%
1949–50	0.25	0.13	0.56	0.03	0.03	0.57	0.12	0.04	0.23	0.05
1955–56	0.13	0.17	0.62	0.04	0.04	0.45	0.18	0.02	0.28	0.06
1959–60	0.13	0.21	0.59	0.04	0.03	0.43	0.25	0.02	0.25	0.05
1965–66	0.14	0.23	0.54	0.03	0.05	0.43	0.30	0.02	0.18	0.06
1969–70	0.15	0.19	0.57	0.03	0.05	0.44	0.26	0.03	0.19	0.08
1975–76	0.16	0.18	0.61	0.03	0.02	0.48	0.25	0.04	0.19	0.04
1979–80	0.15	0.16	0.62	0.04	0.03	0.47	0.25	0.04	0.19	0.05
1985–86	0.18	0.13	0.61	0.05	0.03	0.50	0.22	0.03	0.19	0.06

Note: Does not include revenue from auxiliary enterprises and sales and services.

* Does not include student aid revenues provided by governments. These appear under gross tuition.

Source: Michael McPherson and Morton Schapiro, *Keeping College Affordable: Government's Role in Promoting Educational Opportunity* (Washington, D.C.: 1991).

pertains to students who are residents of that state unless there are reciprocal agreements with other states.

Public institutions are usually larger and have different funding sources. Financial aid offices in the public sector generally have larger staffs, and assignments are often distributed based on various funding programs. However, financial aid officers in both the public and private sectors must be equipped with counseling skills that allow for the successful deployment of whatever resources are available to meet student needs.

Competition?

A growing concern among college and university presidents, as well as enrollment, admission, and financial aid officers, centers on whether low-cost institutions have become "too affordable." That is, whether the tuition differential between the sectors has reached a point where affluent families are being attracted to low-cost public institutions in such numbers that access is limited among lower-income and minority students who participate at a lesser rate to begin with. McPherson and Schapiro (1991) have collected national data that seem to indicate both sectors are competing evenly for needy, low-income students because the net cost after financial aid (mostly in the private sector) is comparable.[1] Private institutions, however, are losing ground in the competition to enroll students from upper-income families because here the net price difference between sectors is significant. If this trend continues, low-cost institutions will have difficulty achieving the goal of access while high-cost institutions will be weakened by the need to subsidize a large portion of the student body. For example, it is not uncommon in some states for community college graduates with solid academic records to find that access to the four-year, public college or university is limited because of the lack of space. This lose-lose scenario is likely to be the central issue for higher education financing in the 1990s, and its resolution will have profound implications for both sectors as well as for admission and financial aid policies and practices.

---

1. McPherson and Schapiro offer some thought-provoking proposals in their recent publication, *Keeping College Affordable* (1991), including the federalizing of all student aid programs and a dramatic increase in public tuitions so that needy students would qualify for federal aid.

Financial Aid: How Much Is Too Much? How Little Is Too Little?

Most ball games are lost, not won.
Casey Stengel

Packaging

It will be helpful to revisit an enrollment management goal mentioned in Chapter 3, *pricing and financial aid strategies:* "to implement pricing and financial aid strategies that will optimize the institution's ability to attract and retain the desired academic, racial/ethnic, and socioeconomic mix of students." To varying degrees, colleges and universities have used financial aid as a tool to meet institutional enrollment goals. The objective typically is to identify and implement an allocation strategy that meets the particular institution's needs within the framework of resources available. These objectives may be quantitative—numbers of students; they may imply diversity— including underrepresented minority students and international students; they may be qualitative—attracting students with a high level of academic ability and preparedness; or they may be fiscal—reflecting the institution's financial circumstances. Sometimes independently, sometimes in conjunction with the admission personnel, financial aid officers have created alternative methods of "packaging" financial assistance to individual students as a way to meet these needs. This is often the case when enrollment management structures are in place. Such packaging usually includes varying the levels of self-help components, that is, loans and work during the academic year, along with grant or scholarship funds. This may or may not be based on an attempt to meet a student's full demonstrated need. There are at least seven common variations on the financial aid packaging theme, as described and briefly evaluated below.

Uniform Self-Help

This strategy provides a constant level of self-help for all students. For example, the aid officer calculates that there are 1,000 students who demonstrate need and that the average need of those students is $10,000. One thousand students at $10,000 average need means that the aggregate need for that class is $10 million. The institution in this hypothetical example has determined that it has approximately $7 million in financial aid resources. Thus, $3 million will be required in self-help, or $3,000 of self-help per person. A typical breakdown might include a loan of $2,000 and student employment (College Work-Study or regular employment) to cover the remaining $1,000.

This is an ideal approach, provided the resources of the institution and the need levels of students are such that a reasonable and competitive self-help package can be created. It is the strategy employed by most institutions that boast of a need-blind admission policy (i.e., the decision to admit a student is made independent of his or her need for financial aid). Many of the strongest institutions in the country, from a competitive admission point of view, employ this approach, including the Ivy League and other prestigious private institutions, and flagship public universities. The demand for places at these institutions far outweighs the supply of available seats, so these institutions are assured adequate representation by students who can pay the cost of attendance as well as those with financial need.

A second institutional type that utilizes this strategy exhibits a much weaker profile from an admission/enrollment perspective. These schools can best be described as unselective. In addition, there is typically little recognition or appreciation of the influence financial aid can have on the matriculation decision, nor is there understanding of the price sensitivity of the market. These institutions are vulnerable from a competitive point of view and may well fall short of their enrollment objectives with this approach.

Uniform self-help is insensitive to *levels* of need because everyone receives a set amount of loan and work monies, regardless of whether they need $6,000 or $14,000 to meet the student budget. This approach is also insensitive to academic quality. Students with very strong academic backgrounds are treated exactly the same as those with weaker backgrounds. This is less a problem for a high-demand institution because these institutions don't have to distinguish between the academic quality and the financial needs of their population. They are dealing at the very high end of the quality continuum and everyone admitted has, for instance, above 1200 on the SAT and is from the top 10 percent of the high school graduating class. The more vulnerable, less-selective institution has a very wide quality band, from the academic superstar to those who have demonstrated far less academic ability, have low standardized test scores, and anchor the bottom part of the class. Uniform self-help in this case, which some would argue is fair, misses an opportunity to benefit the institution through deployment of student aid to the academically more able.

Uniform self-help is also consistent with the land-grant mission of public institutions and the goal of treating all citizens of the state in a consistent fashion. Those citizens (students) are entitled to go to a state institution and that entitlement appropriately includes comparable levels of self-help which, of course, guarantee equal debt burdens.

Self-Help Varied by Ability to Borrow

This is the most need-sensitive approach. It requires that, within the newly admitted or enrolled population, students are treated differently in terms of the proportion of loan and work each receives in their financial aid package (based on their overall financial need). This approach may be employed by an institution that does not want a needy person to borrow beyond a certain limit. This approach may stem from institutional research demonstrating that students at a certain income and need level become so encumbered with debt that they don't survive four years. Alternatively, it may be found that students at a certain need level will refuse offers of admission if the loan component is too large. Although this approach is sensitive to need, it is not sensitive to quality in that a very highly qualified student, who might well be in demand at other institutions, could receive a less attractive financial aid package (more self-help) if her/his need was deemed to be at a modest level.

Self-Help Varied by Desirability

"Desirability" here refers to the overall attractiveness of the candidate. This alternative is need insensitive, but quality sensitive. Thus, in employing this strategy, the institution would take the "superstar" and give that person a financial aid package with a very low self-help component, perhaps $1,000 or $2,000. A more typical "bread-and-butter" student may be offered more in self-help, perhaps the institutional average of $3,000. Finally, the person who is the least desirable or attractive candidate would be offered a still higher self-help component of $4,000. This is really an attempt to manipulate the applicant pool by treating those who are considered at a premium—based on high ability—in such a way as to increase their likelihood of enrollment. Those not at a premium (i.e., there are a large number of them in the applicant pool and they typically enroll at a fairly high rate) need no special treatment.

Self-Help Varied by Ability to Borrow and Desirability

With this approach, the financial aid process starts to become quite complex, but a matrix can be created which dictates that if a student is at a certain quality level (high), and a certain need level (high), one self-help package is awarded; if at a high-quality, low-need level, a different self-help package is created; if in a low-quality, high-need quadrant, yet another package would be offered, as shown in Figure 5.

	Low Quality High Need	High Quality High Need	
Self-Help = $4,000			Self-Help = $2,000
Self-Help = $3,000	Low Quality Low Need	High Quality Low Need	Self-Help = $3,000

FIGURE 5. Need/Quality Matrix

A given institution's accepted applicant pool will dictate both the definition of quality and the definition of need. Also, the behavior of an institution's applicant pool will dictate appropriate levels of self-help. If the average that the institution can afford is $3,000, it will be necessary for the number of high-quality, high-need students enrolling to be equal to the number of low-quality, high-need students enrolling in order to keep financial aid expenditures in line. This approach, as well as all the others, is institutionally driven. For example, if an institution's average scholarship award is too high, then one of the goals may be to reduce that average. The strategy then may call for giving priority to low-need applicants by offering them an attractive self-help package to increase their rate of enrollment, but still with a lower-than-average scholarship award.

Admit/Deny

This is a more traditional approach to the allocation of a fixed financial aid budget. In this scenario, an institution knows prior to making its aid awards, or discovers at some point in the process, that the budget allocated is insufficient to meet the full need of all students. Self-help is set at what is determined to be a reasonable and competitive level, with the understanding that funds will be exhausted prior to filling the class. For instance, if an institution desires to enroll 1,000 needy students and the institutional aid budget has been set at $6 million, and if the institution further believes that to be competitive its average self-help for most students should exceed $3,000, then that would be the package offered to the first 857 enrollees. At that rate, the aid budget will be exhausted, and the class will be 143 short of target. The remaining needy students would be accepted but denied institutional aid. In all likelihood, the matriculation rate of these last students would drop substantially, and the admission officer would thus need to admit lower in the applicant pool to fill the class. If overall an institution has had a 50 percent yield on needy students (i.e., 50 percent of admitted needy students actually enroll), under an admit-deny financial aid strategy, the yield could drop to 20 percent or lower for this last group. Interestingly, it would not drop to zero. Although this strategy would keep the financial aid budget in balance for that first year, it has been the experience of most institutions that the admit-deny enrollees become frequent visitors to the financial aid office in their upper-class years and that eventually institutional funds are awarded to these students.

Aid-Conscious Admission

Basing admission decisions at least partly on whether a student needs financial aid is regarded by some as a much more unfair way to manage institutional aid allocation and meet enrollment goals. Others will argue, however, that this is ultimately a much more equitable approach. There is logic to both sides of the argument and people tend to feel strongly both ways, one side claiming that it is totally unfair to make an admission decision based on ability to pay, those opposed decrying the "crudeness" of accepting high-need students knowing full well that they will not receive any institutional aid dollars once enrolled. To show how the process works, we will go back to our previous example. Once the 857 students were awarded financial aid packages and enrolled, the last 143 spaces would go not to the next most qualified in the pool, some of whom were needy, but to those who either did not apply for financial aid or applied and demonstrated no need. Once again this requires the admission office to dig lower in the applicant pool and, in some cases, to exhaust all applicants who have the ability to meet the cost of attendance. These last two approaches have the potential liability of turning off future generations of needy applicants who conclude from these policies that the institution is unfriendly to students who demonstrate need.

Merit Awards

This is a different approach than the previous six, primarily because the others focused on the need-based population. The art of managing an institutional aid budget while at the same time meeting enrollment goals has become increasingly challenging at many institutions. Merit scholarships allow institutions to increase the numbers enrolling who receive less institutional aid than might be necessary for the average needy student. Thus, if more students enroll with a $5,000 merit award and replace a similar number of needy students with an average $7,000 financial aid requirement, then the makeup of the class will change qualitatively and the institution will spend less on average per new student. There are many downsides to this approach, not the least of which is trying to identify students who would not enroll without the merit award. That is the subject of the next chapter.

Renewals

Up until now, we have been discussing financial aid strategies aimed at first-time students. Packaging for returning students is a different exercise.

How returning students are treated in their upper-class years tends to be an institutionally specific, often budget-driven, decision. Variations range from triage (only increase institutional funds if absolutely necessary), to a uniform increase in self-help by class with additional aid in the form of institutional grants to meet need, to "gapping" (creating financial aid packages that leave a specified amount of need unmet). Few institutions have done research to determine the impact of financial aid policies and practices on retention. Inadequate financial aid tends to be an easy "fall guy" when students are asked why they are leaving a particular institution. The reasons are usually more complex, and financial aid may or may not play a role.

Other Approaches

There is still another set of popular approaches, some of which are merely variations of previously described strategies, known as equity, differential, and preferential packaging.

Equity packaging. With equity packaging, all students are treated similarly. Uniform self-help is, in fact, a form of equity packaging. The other two forms are "gapping" an equal dollar amount for each student, or meeting a fixed percent of need for each student. For example, to return again to our 1,000 students with $10,000 average need, if the aid budget is $6 million and the best self-help is determined to be $3,000 on average, the institution might just "gap" all students by $1,000. This has the effect of raising self-help by another $1,000 but not providing students and families access to funds, be they loan or work. It could, of course, have a detrimental effect on rates of enrollment, which would require the admission office to dig lower into the pool of candidates to fill the class. This approach is insensitive to quality, but not insensitive to need. The high-need person would have no more of a gap to fill than the low-need person, assuming that self-help is the first component of the package introduced after the family contribution is applied toward the cost of education.

Meeting a fixed percentage of need, for example, meeting 90 percent of all need as opposed to 100 percent, is also quality insensitive, but has the added attribute of being need sensitive in a manner that taxes the neediest most severely. For example, if an accepted applicant needed $5,000 to enroll and 90 percent of need was being met under this form of equity packaging, then the total aid package would be $4,500, leaving a gap of $500. If another student needed $10,000 to enroll, at the 90 percent level, $9,000 would be the total aid package, leaving a gap of $1,000. This approach could lower the enrollment rates of accepted high-need candidates.

Differential and preferential packaging. These are really variations on the "desirability" approach described earlier. Differential packaging requires that individuals receive different levels of self-help based on their overall attractiveness as applicants, as defined by the institution. Preferential packaging requires treating groups of people differently based on their profile (e.g., underrepresented minority students, alumni children, athletes). Basically, these two approaches have a common goal—to increase the enrollment rate of students perceived to be at a premium in the applicant pool.

With the exception of the first two approaches, namely uniform self-help and self-help varied by ability to borrow, the remaining strategies, when measured against the principles and practices of student financial aid cited in Chapter 2, create varying degrees of conflict and even contradiction for the financial aid officer. Balancing the needs of the institution versus the needs of the individual, as we have said, is an ongoing juggling act for many in the financial aid profession. Each approach has significant admission implications that affect the makeup of the class by quality, ethnicity, and affluence, as well as the extent to which the institution can be selective. There are no clear-cut solutions except for those few prestigious institutions that are able to meet enrollment goals with existing resources. An educated guess would place perhaps only 6 percent of the colleges and universities in the country in this advantaged position.

Creative Management of Institutional Aid Budgets

In many college and university accounting systems, financial aid is appropriately listed as an expenditure item; in others it is with equal propriety netted against revenues since the effect is clearly the same. In fact, it is common for chief financial officers to monitor and even manage financial aid budgets as a percentage of tuition income. With the doubling and even tripling of institutional aid budgets over the course of the 1980s, many institutions have set a goal of capping financial aid as a percentage of tuition income. This is an appropriate practice to follow *if* the institution is at its ideal enrollment. "Ideal" enrollment is defined here as the maximum number of students that can be enrolled without having to significantly add to the fixed cost base of the institution (e.g., additional facilities, equipment, faculty, staff, etc.). If excess capacity exists, that is, if students could be added without any significant increase in fixed costs, then managing the financial aid budget as a percentage of tuition income is probably inappropriate and possibly counterproductive. Capping financial aid as a percentage of tuition income is likely to have the effect of reducing net tuition revenues if excess capacity exists.

By way of example, let's look at T.M.L.A.U. (Traditional Midwestern Liberal Arts University). Assume the ideal enrollment for T.M.L.A.U. is 1,200 students. The university aid budget for 1991–92 has been set at $5 million. Tuition in 1991–92 is $14,500. A goal has been set to keep the percentage of tuition and fee income committed to scholarship aid at less than 30 percent. That's how the $5 million financial aid budget was set. Question: Should the admission and financial aid offices live within the financial aid budget and enroll only 1,160 students or should they exceed the aid budget and meet the ideal enrollment?

Scenario One

In keeping with the dictum that scholarships should represent less than 30 percent of tuition income, which yields the $5 million financial aid budget, the admission and financial aid offices believe they can enroll 290 new students, freshman and transfer, and 870 continuing students for a total of 1,160. Multiplying the 1991–92 tuition of $14,500 by 1,160 produces $16,820,000 of gross revenue. Subtracting $5 million of financial aid expenditure leaves $11,820,000 net tuition revenue. Financial aid therefore represents 29.7 percent of tuition income.

Scenario Two

For an extra $400,000 of institutional aid, the admission and financial aid offices believe they can enroll 300 new students and 900 continuing students for a total of 1,200. That student population times the tuition of $14,500 produces gross tuition revenues of $17,400,000. When the $5.4 million financial aid budget is subtracted, net tuition revenues are $12 million, or $180,000 higher than in the first scenario. Because the ideal enrollment has been met there are no additional fixed costs. Thus the $180,000 additional tuition revenue is new net income to the university. The percentage of tuition income going to scholarship aid, however, has grown from 29.7 percent to 31 percent.

There are other ancillary benefits to meeting the ideal enrollment, such as:

a. there are more students on campus, which creates the potential for a better educational environment;

b. there is better utilization of the residence halls with additional revenue of $90,000 (40 × $2,250);

c. there are fewer withdrawals by continuing students who could not otherwise afford T.M.L.A.U.;

d. there are lower per unit costs for dining; and

e. there is a larger enrollment base to build upon for enrollment in subsequent years.

All of the above demonstrate that financial aid and admission officers have the potential to play critical roles in fundamental institutional decisions. Although the admission officer is frequently recognized as part of an institutional "first team," which includes the chief academic officer, the chief executive officer, and the chief financial officer, only very recently and only at very few institutions has the financial aid officer been asked to join the party. (We should note, however, that the foregoing is a moot point at public institutions, except where state funding is increased or decreased depending upon the institution's ability to meet a certain enrollment target. Typically, public institutions are not in a position to allocate institutional aid in the way described in this example.)

During the 1980s, a number of creative student employment programs were initiated in an attempt to attract highly qualified and motivated students. Cornell, Rochester, Duke, and about 30 other institutions supported by the Charles Dana Foundation developed and implemented such programs. Basically they sought to reward outstanding students who wanted to "work their way through college" by offering them educationally purposeful, career-related employment opportunities which, through wages earned and additional scholarship assistance, reduced the level of borrowing or family contribution necessary to meet the cost of attendance. These additional funds were often raised through donations from alumni and friends, but also, in some cases, from the institutional aid budget. The latter case has frequently been cited as a better use of institutional funds than direct grant or scholarship awards because it has had a more positive effect on matriculation and retention.

Finally, we find institutions investing in family loan programs, monthly payment plans, and even prepayment plans—all addressing the issue of affordability.

Programs that Work in Reverse

Given the complexity surrounding financial aid and the variety of strategies employed at U.S. colleges and universities, it is not surprising that some aid programs can backfire—actually discouraging students the institution would like to enroll. To illustrate the point, if an institution has an alumni scholarship program, as many in the country do, and, historically, alumni have felt it a privilege or requirement to screen and choose candidates for this scholarship, a program intended to assist in the enrollment of the best students could, in fact, have just the opposite effect. For example, if, in a given alumni region, 50 candidates are nominated for the alumni scholarship, but only five scholarships are available, an expectation will have been created among all 50 but 45 will be disappointed. If the quality of all 50 candidates is such that the institution desires to enroll the maximum number, the alumni scholarship program could be a detriment to reaching that objective.

As another example, many institutions have what can best be called "categorical" scholarships, that is, a fixed number of scholarships designated to encourage the application and enrollment of a certain type of student (graduates of Jesuit high schools, students who plan to participate in debate, students with particular artistic talent, etc.). Once again, if an expectation is created by the promotion and publication of these fixed scholarships, or if the number of candidates who judge themselves eligible far exceeds the number of scholarships available, the implication for those not chosen can once again be dashed expectations. If these disappointed students are desirable and the institution wants to maximize enrollment by these applicants, this scholarship program too could have a detrimental effect. In many cases a real "Catch 22" is at work, in that students who are not chosen for these categorical scholarships are treated just like other applicants and, in fact, could receive very substantial need-based or perhaps even merit scholarship packages. The financial aid outcome for these applicants in fact may not be substantially different, or not different at all from what it would have been with the categorical scholarship, and yet they are likely to feel less positive about themselves and about the institution that wants to enroll them.

A final concern is with "full-tuition scholarships." A number of colleges and universities across the country have for some time sponsored and conducted full-tuition scholarship programs. If, as is the case at most institutions, there's a need to maximize net tuition revenue, this approach is counterproductive. Typically, institutions with these programs have never tested whether the full-tuition approach is necessary to matriculate the candidates they desire. They have merely assumed that, to get the very best of whatever category of students they seek, the full-tuition approach is required. It is, of course, also a very clean and neat package. Assume, for instance, that quality is a concern at an institution. The traditional full-tuition scholarship produces a dozen superstars each year (i.e., students from the top 1 or 2 percent of their high school graduating classes with SATS in the stratosphere, above 1400). These scholarships are an expense. If tuition is $10,000, then the cost of full scholarships per class is

$120,000, or $480,000 over an undergraduate career. Assume that half-tuition scholarships could guarantee enrollment of two dozen very good, but not superstar, students (top 5 percent of their high school graduating classes and SATS above 1200). For the same expense, 24 of these students could be enrolled while, at the same time, producing net revenues of $120,000 per class, or $480,000 over the course of an undergraduate career. Given the vagaries of the admission process and the fact that predicting success in college is an art as well as a science, the appropriateness of full-tuition scholarship programs certainly should be reviewed.

Strategy Summary

All these approaches to the creative management of enrollment can best be described as a series of trade-offs—involving money, quality, and numbers of students, or "yield." What's important is that the trade-offs be well informed; that the institution have a good sense of itself, of its needs, and of its purpose in serving students. The implications of trade-offs, what's gained and what's lost, must be institutionally specific. The perceived value or worth of a particular undergraduate experience by a student and her or his family cannot be ascertained from national norms, industry standards, or sectorwide experience. Each institution must study and evaluate its financial aid and admission policies and practices and understand the impact each has on meeting its enrollment goals. There are no quick fixes. There are no easy answers. Nonetheless, Chapter 6 will provide some direction and suggestions on how institutions can approach these issues.

Targeting Financial Aid to Enrollment Goals

It's what you learn after you know it all that counts.
Earl Weaver

Unfortunately, to focus on strategic deployment of financial aid is attending to a solution, not to the problem. The problem is the desirability or the value of the product—the undergraduate educational experience at our colleges and universities—and the price that is charged to sustain that effort. If the product, the institutionally specific undergraduate education, is not viewed as being worth the value, families are unlikely to pay the cost, whether it's the "sticker price" or some reduced price resulting from financial assistance. Thus first and foremost, institutions should be constantly focused on improving the quality of the undergraduate experience. The higher the perceived value, the more students and families, as well as the government, will be willing to pay. This chapter will focus on identifying ways of determining the price sensitivity of students and their families with regard to a particular institution as well as how to craft financial aid solutions to meet that level of price sensitivity.

Calculating Enrollment Yields

To begin, admission and aid offices need to have merged data files so that full admission and financial aid information on each individual applicant is integrated and available. Figure 6 shows the way the data must be integrated.

In Figure 6, applications are defined as all freshman applicants. That population is then segmented into those who applied for financial aid by whatever definition an institution uses (an indication on the admission application of a desire to apply, the receipt of a need analysis form, or the filing of an institutional financial aid application). The remaining applicants are then grouped as non-aid applicants. Clearly, the sum of the two must equal all freshman applicants. On the left-hand side of the diagram, under aid applicants, there are five possible institutional responses to the application for admission and financial aid.

1. admission acceptance and a need-based financial aid award;

2. admission acceptance, no financial need demonstrated, no financial aid award;

3. admission acceptance, financial need demonstrated, no financial aid award;

4. admission acceptance, no financial need demonstrated, a merit award;

5. rejection of admission.

The sum of the five categories should equal all financial aid applicants. Non-aid applicants include:

1. admission acceptance and no aid offered;

2. admission acceptance and merit award offered;

3. rejection of admission.

Once again, the three categories are the only possibilities for the disposition of the admission applications and their sum must equal all non-aid applicants.

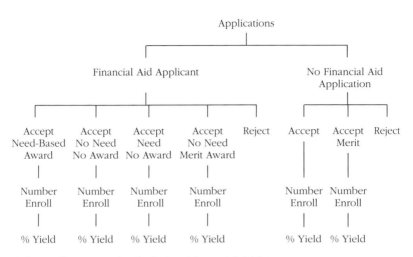

FIGURE 6.   Merged Admission/Financial Aid Data

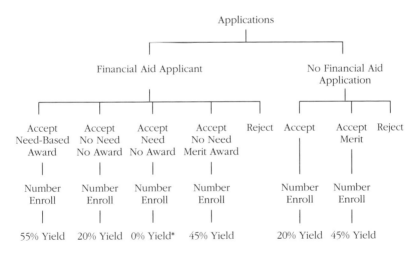

FIGURE 7.   Yield Calculation by Aid Group
* 0% yield because no one was in this category.

A subgroup of those in each accepted category then enroll and a yield can be calculated for each group as indicated in Figure 7. In calculating the yields for each category, it is clear that enrollment rates are lower among those who were accepted and who applied for aid but did not receive it and among those who were accepted but never applied for aid and received no merit award. The difference in yields of 25 to 35 percentage points identifies an area of opportunity for an institution to exploit. The institution can then examine the profiles of students in those categories to determine whether rates of enrollment could be increased if some discounting or merit funds were made available to such groups.

This exercise can be expanded into longitudinal studies over a three- to five-year period to determine whether the distribution of applicants has changed. For example, if Institution A experienced a decline in applications from 7,000 to 5,000 over a three-year period, where did the losses occur? If it was originally assumed that the decline was approximately 50/50 or 1,000 each between aid applicants and non-aid applicants applying for admission, but a study reveals that the loss came entirely from the non-aid applicant pool, the implications for the admission office would be significant. Those responsible for recruitment could examine their policies and practices to determine whether their messages were being misread. For instance, too heavy an emphasis on affordability for needy students could give the impression to the public at large that only low- and middle-income students were welcome at the institution. The overall success of financial aid and merit scholarship programs can also be monitored and tracked with this approach.

Finally, Figure 8 describes how the results of this exercise might be strategically implemented. For example, assume that there were 150 students, in the two categories that produced 20 percent yields, whose quality placed them just outside the institution's merit aid program (e.g., they had combined SAT scores of 1000 to 1200). It would be possible to conduct an experiment with these groups. The 150 students are divided evenly into three groups of 50. One group is treated as the control and no aid is offered. Typically, 10 of them will enroll for a 20 percent yield. The second group is offered $1,500 merit awards to see if yield can be increased. And finally, the third group is offered $3,000 merit awards to see if the yield can be increased even further. If we assume tuition is $10,000, the 10 enrollees in the control group produce $100,000 tuition income, be-

	Q 1000–1200*		
Students	50	50	50
Aid Awarded	0	$1,500	$3,000
Enrollees (increase)	10	15 (+5)	20 (+10)
Yield (percent)	20%	30%	40%
Tuition Revenue	$100,000 (net = gross)	$127,500 −100,000	$140,000 −100,000
Additional Net Tuition	0	$27,500	$40,000

*"Quality" measure based on SAT scores.

FIGURE 8. Merit Aid Experiment (150 in Population)

cause net and gross tuition income are the same. In group two, if 15 students enroll at a net tuition of $8,500, then the total net tuition revenue for that group is $127,500, or $27,500 greater than the control group. And finally, in group three, with a net tuition of $7,000, if 20 students enroll for a 40 percent yield, then the total net for that group is $140,000, or $40,000 more than the control group. Thus by studying the behavior of students in the applicant pool and experimenting with merit aid or discounts based on segmentation by quality, new policies can be crafted to increase both enrollments of certain groups and net revenues.

More Empirical Research

Some further hypotheses to be tested could include the following:

a. With self-help constant, yield will decrease with increasing need because poorer families will have a more difficult time making up the difference and perhaps place a lower premium on the value of an education.

b. With self-help constant, yield will be constant with increasing need since a true need analysis takes all factors into account in determining ability to pay. (Large numbers of applicants over a period of time should provide the operational definition of ability to pay.) Or,

c. With self-help constant, yield will increase with increasing need. This could be true for sociological reasons—poorer families make greater sacrifices. It could also be true for psychological reasons—the simple attraction of more money offered will increase yield. This type of study must be conducted institution by institution.

Typically, as quality increases, yield decreases; as aid increases, yield increases; and as need increases, yield increases. The matrices in Tables 8 through 11—quality by need; need by aid award; quality by merit award; and finally, need by aid award at a given quality level—can help an institution test these hypotheses with its own applicants. In all four matrices, yield equals matriculations divided by acceptances.

"Quality" can be defined in any number of ways. Traditional criteria include admission rating, combined SAT scores, ACT scores, grade-point average, and rank in class. Other characteristics considered might be racial/ethnic group, alumni children, etc., whoever is at a premium in the applicant pool. For purposes of illustration, combined SAT scores are used in these examples. On the need and award axes, it is best to start with a zero column and then use increments of one thousand dollars (e.g., $1–1,000; $1,101–2,000; etc.). In all likelihood it will be necessary to combine these cells once the population being studied has been distributed. However, because it is impossible to predict in advance what the distribution will be or how the population will group around certain quality-and-need or quality-and-aid award levels, it is advisable to start by using a highly segmented approach.

Tables 12 and 13 demonstrate the kind of research outcome that gives an institution the opportunity to react strategically in the use of financial aid. For example, in Table 12, at a comparable quality level of between 1100 and 1200 combined SAT scores, we see behavior differences among those students who received either no award or less than $3,001; those who received between $3,001 and $4,000; and those who received more than $4,000 in aid. Clearly, higher awards (above $5,000) seem to make little difference, so that could be set as the ceiling for an institutional aid award because larger

TABLE 8. Quality by Need

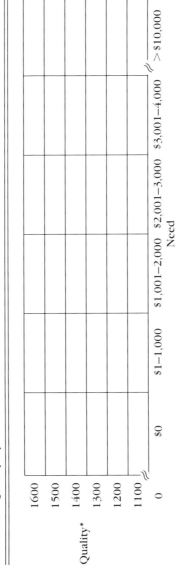

Quality*	$0	$1–1,000	$1,001–2,000	$2,001–3,000	$3,001–4,000	>$10,000
1600						
1500						
1400						
1300						
1200						
1100						

Need

* Combined SAT score.

TABLE 9.   Need by Aid Award

Aid	$0	$1–1,000	$1,001–2,000	$2,001–3,000	$3,001–4,000	> $20,000
> $20,000						
$3,001–4,000						
$2,001–3,000						
$1,001–2,000						
$1–1,000						
$0						

Need

TABLE 10. Quality by Merit Award

Quality	$1–1,000	$1,001–2,000	$2,001–3,000	$3,001–4,000	$4,001–5,000	>$20,000
>1500						
1400–1499						
1300–1399						
1200–1299						
1100–1199						
1000–1099						
900–999						
800–899						
400–499						
0						

Merit Award

TABLE 11. Need by Aid Award at a Given Quality Level (Quality = 1001–1100)

Aid Awarded	$0	$1–1,000	$1,001–2,000	$2,001–3,000	$3,001–4,000	$4,001–5,000	>$20,000
>$20,000							
$4,001–5,000							
$3,001–4,000							
$2,001–3,000							
$1,001–2,000							
$1–1,000							
$0							

Need

TABLE 12. Quality by Aid Award

Quality	$1–1,000	$1,001–2,000	$2,001–3,000	$3,001–4,000	$4,001–5,000	$5,001–6,000	$6,001–7,000	$7,001–8,000	>$20,000
1600									
1500									
1400									
1300									
1200									
1100		3/18	3/18	3/9	5/10	4/8	3/6	1/2	
1000									
0									

Aid Award

TABLE 13. Aid Awarded by Need at a Given Quality Level (Quality = 1100–1200)

*Yield

Aid Award	$0	$1–1,000	$1,001–2,000	$2,001–3,000	$3,001–4,000	$4,001–5,000	$5,001–6,000	$\approx$ >$20,000
$10,000								
$9,000								
$8,000								
$7,000						.50		
$6,000						.47		
$5,000						.45		
$4,000						.45		
$3,000						.20		
$2,000						.15		
$1,000						.10		
$0						.05		

Need

*Yield = matriculants ÷ need.

awards will not increase the likelihood of matriculation. The next decision is whether a $3,000 award at a 33 percent yield is satisfactory or whether spending another $1,000 per applicant, increasing the yield to 50 percent, is preferable. Table 13 shows that at a given quality level, 1100–1200 combined SAT scores and top 10 percent of the class, students with financial need between $4,001 and $5,000 have a much greater likelihood of enrollment if their need is met; this does not substantially increase with awards beyond need. Thus awards above need at this quality level don't appear to be a productive utilization of institutional resources. In this type of research, aid is defined as free dollars to the student—grant or scholarship money regardless of source (federal, state, or institutional) but not self-help (work and loans). It may also be necessary, once the "free dollar to the student" research has been conducted, to do a similar study of those institutional funds over which the aid office, or the aid and admission office, exercises total discretion.

It is important to stress that the focus here is on the strategic deployment of institutional resources to meet a particular institution's enrollment goal. Simply stated, this type of research focuses on looking for differences in behavior among like groups or groups that have previously been treated in a like fashion. Institutional opportunities lie in the identification of these differences. This is where the strategic deployment of financial aid can make the biggest difference. Another term for this activity is "management by fact," where financial aid is seen as a resource of an institution to help meet its admission and enrollment goals. Only by conducting analysis and evaluation can admission and aid offices be confident that institutional dollars are being targeted to those students most likely to respond and that the recruitment of these students will assist in meeting institutional enrollment objectives.

Conclusions and Recommendations

The game's not over until it's over.
Yogi Berra

The goal of this monograph was to look at historical developments in financial aid and their impact on admission and enrollment at U.S. colleges and universities, as well as to look at where things are today in the last decade of the century, and where they are likely to go. There is, to be sure, much more that can be said about financial aid, pricing, admission, retention, and enrollment. However, five major concerns have emerged which will require the attention of aid administrators, admission officers, chief executive officers, and public officials as we look to the future.

1. Traditional funding sources for students in higher education have either reached maximum capacity or are dangerously close to it. There will likely be a need for a new system of funding. This could take the form of new partners, e.g., corporations, and new modes of learning, e.g., expanded cooperative education. It could even take the form of a new approach to financing education such as the "federalizing" of student aid, as suggested by McPherson and Schapiro (1991).

2. Public policy regarding the dual system needs to be reexamined. Our system of higher education is falling into disrepair because of the growing tuition differential between the public and private sectors. Access is becoming limited in the public sector and financial viability is a serious concern in the private sector.

3. Financial aid and admission professionals should be involved from initial consultation through final decision making in the setting of price, both gross and net, at private institutions and should serve as expert witnesses for public officials whose responsibility it is to establish price at state-supported colleges and universities.

4. Each institution has to understand how it is perceived in the market. What is its value? How much are people willing to pay for that particular undergraduate educational experience? From that understanding can emerge a series of strategic responses, including admission criteria, recruitment programs, product development/enhancement, and improved financial aid deployment.

5. The financial aid profession need not and should not abandon its principles and practices because of market competition. On the contrary, reaffirming the most important principles, practices, and policies, and working hard to reach outcomes consistent with those ideals, should be the task at hand. The challenges will be many, the decisions difficult, but if that were not the case, there would be no need for principles, practices, and attendant policies.

> **There are three types of baseball players:**
> **—those who make it happen**
> **—those who watch it happen**
> **—those who wonder what happens.**
> **Tommy Lasorda**

References

Astin, Alexander W. 1975. "Financial Aid and Student Persistence." In *Preventing Students from Dropping Out.* Chapters 3 and 8. Higher Education Research Report Series 1975, 3–24. San Francisco: Jossey-Bass.

Benezet, Louis T. 1976. *Private Higher Educational Public Funding.* Washington, D.C.: ERIC Higher Education Research Report No. 5.

Bowen, Howard R. 1976. "Where the Numbers Fail." In *Individualizing the System.* San Francisco: Jossey-Bass, 8–17.

Bowen, William G. 1968. *The Economics of the Major Private Universities.* Berkeley, Calif.: Carnegie Commission on Higher Education.

Bowen, William G. 1987. *The Student Aid/Tuition Nexus.* Unpublished paper.

Bowman, James L. 1970. *Some Thoughts and Reflections Regarding Parental Ability to Pay for Higher Education.* New York: College Entrance Examination Board.

College Board. 1991. *Manual for Student Aid Administrators: Policies and Procedures.* New York: College Entrance Examination Board.

Doermann, Humphrey. 1978. *Toward Equal Access.* New York: College Entrance Examination Board.

References

Ehrenberg, Ronald G., and Daniel S. Sherman. 1984. "Optimal Financial Aid Policies for a Selective University." *Journal of Human Resources.* Vol. 19, No. 2: 202–230.

Elliott, William. 1975. *The Management of Admissions and Financial Aid: The Net Tuition Concept.* Unpublished doctoral thesis. University of Michigan Microfiche Library.

Farago, Peter T. 1978. "Assession, The Effectiveness and Propriety of Merit-Based Scholarships." From the Proceedings of *Institutional Research: New Responses to New Demands.* Northeast Association of Institutional Research, October: 279–285.

Fife, Jonathan D. 1975. *The College Student Grant Study.* University Park, Pa.: Penn State University Press.

Fife, Jonathan D., and Larry Leslie. 1975. "The College Student Grant Study." *The Journal of Higher Education.* Vol. XLV, No. 9: 651–671.

Fife, Jonathan D., Larry Leslie, and Gary Johnson. 1975. "The College Student Grant Study: A Reply." *The Journal of Higher Education.* Vol. XLVI, No. 5, September/October: 607–609.

Finn, Chester E., Jr. 1978. *Scholars, Dollars, and Bureaucrats.* Washington, D.C.: Brookings Institution.

Finn, Chester E., Jr. 1985. "Why Do We Need Financial Aid? or, Desanctifying Student Assistance." In *An Agenda for the Year 2000.* New York: College Entrance Examination Board.

Gillespie, Donald A., and Nancy Carlson. 1983. *Trends in Student Aid: 1963 to 1983.* Washington, D.C.: College Entrance Examination Board.

Gladieux, Lawrence, and Janet Hansen. 1990. *Trends in Student Aid 1980 to 1990.* Washington, D.C.: College Entrance Examination Board.

Glover, Stephen. 1978. "The Middle Income Squeeze." *The Journal of Student Financial Aid.* Vol. 8, No. 1, March.

Hansen, Janet S. 1990. *College Savings Plans.* New York: College Entrance Examination Board.

Hansen, Janet S., and Lawrence E. Gladieux. 1978. *Middle Income Students: A New Target for Federal Aid?* New York: College Entrance Examination Board.

Hossler, Don. 1984. *Enrollment Management: An Integrated Approach.* New York: College Entrance Examination Board.

Jackson, Gregory A. 1978. "Financial Aid and Student Enrollment." *The Journal of Higher Education.* Vol. 49, No. 6, November/December: 548–574.

Jackson, Gregory A., and George B. Weathersby. 1975. "Individual Demand for Higher Education." *Journal of Higher Education.* Vol. XLVI, No. 6, November/December: 623–652.

References

Leslie, Larry. 1977. *Higher Education Opportunity: A Decade of Progress.* Washington, D.C.: ERIC Higher Education Research Report No. 3.

Leslie, Larry L., and Paul T. Brinkman. 1988. *The Economic Value of Higher Education.* New York: American Council on Education and Macmillan Publishing Company.

Leslie, Larry L., and Paul T. Brinkman. 1987. "Student Price Response in Higher Education." *Journal of Higher Education.* Vol. 58, No. 2, March/April: 181–204.

Maguire, John. 1976. "To the Organized Go the Students." *Boston College Bridge Magazine.* Vol. XXXIX, No. 1, Fall: 16–20.

Maguire, John J. 1978. *Financial Aid and the Middle Income Squeeze—Institutional Research, New Response to New Demands.* College Park, Pa.: Northeast Association of Institutional Research.

McNamara, William. 1978. "Washington—The Tax Credit Debate." *Change Magazine.* March: 44, 45, and 60.

McPherson, Michael S. 1988. *How Can We Tell if Federal Student Aid Is Working?* Washington, D.C.: College Entrance Examination Board.

McPherson, Michael S., and Morton O. Schapiro. 1991. *Keeping College Affordable: Government's Role in Promoting Educational Opportunity.* Washington, D.C.: Brookings Institution.

McPherson, Michael S., and Morton O. Schapiro. 1991. "The Student Finance System for Undergraduate Education: How Well Does it Work?" *Change Magazine.* May/June: 16–22.

Minter, John W. 1979. "Current Economic Trends in American Higher Education." *Change Magazine.* February: 19–25.

National Commission on the Financing of Postsecondary Education. 1973. *Financing Postsecondary Education in the U.S.* Washington, D.C.: U.S. Government Printing Office.

National Task Force on Student Aid Problems. 1975. *The Keppel Commission Report* (Final Draft). Washington, D.C.: U.S. Government Printing Office, March.

Nelson, J. Van Duren, and Jacobson. 1978. *The Willingness of Parents to Contribute to Postsecondary Educational Expenses.* New York: College Entrance Examination Board.

Scannell, James J. *The Development of Optimal Financial Aid Strategies.* 1980. University of Michigan Microfiche Library. Unpublished doctoral dissertation.

Schapiro, Morton O., Michael P. O'Mally, and Larry H. Litten. 1990. *Tracing the Economic Backgrounds of COFHE Students: Has There Been a Middle-Income Melt?* Cambridge, Mass.: COFHE.

References

Sidar, Alexander G., Jr. 1976. *No-Need Awards: An Issue.* Paper presented to the College Board College Scholarship Assembly membership. New York: October.

Sidar, Alexander G., Jr., and David A. Potter. 1978. *No-Need/Merit Awards: A Survey of Their Use at Four-Year Public and Private Colleges and Universities.* New York: College Entrance Examination Board.

Silber, John R. 1978–79. "The Tuition Advance Fund: A Proposal for Funding Higher Education." *The College Board Review.* No. 110, Winter: 20, 22–26.

Silber, John R. 1976. "Financing the Independent Sector." In *Individualizing the System.* San Francisco: Jossey-Bass, 107–117.

Spies, Richard R. 1978. *The Effect of Rising Costs on College Choice: A Study of the Application Decision of High Ability Students.* New York: College Entrance Examination Board.

Spies, Richard R. 1990. *The Effect of Rising Costs on College Choice: The Third in a Series of Studies on this Subject.* Princeton, N.J.: Princeton University Press.

Tierney, Michael L., and Jerry S. Davis. 1985. "The Impact of Student Financial Aid and Institutional Net Price on the College Choice Decision of In-State Services." *Journal of Student Financial Aid.* Vol. 15, No. 1, Winter: 3–20.

Weathersby, George B. 1975. "The College Student Grant Study: A Comment." *The Journal of Higher Education.* Vol. XLVI, No. 5, September/October: 601–606.

Weathersby, George B. 1976. "Institutional vs. Student Aid." In *Individualizing the System.* San Francisco: Jossey-Bass, 118–129.